Roald Amundsen and
Robert Scott

Race to the
South Pole

Roald Amundsen
and
Robert Scott

Race to the
South Pole

By Gare Thompson

NATIONAL GEOGRAPHIC

WASHINGTON, D.C.

Founded in 1888, the National Geographic Society is one of the largest nonprofit scientific and educational organizations in the world. It reaches more than 285 million people worldwide each month through its official journal, NATIONAL GEOGRAPHIC, and its four other magazines; the National Geographic Channel; television documentaries; radio programs; films; books; videos and DVDs; maps; and interactive media. National Geographic has funded more than 8,000 scientific research projects and supports an education program combating geographic illiteracy.

For more information, please call
1-800-NGS-LINE (647-5463) or write to the following address:

National·Geographic Society
1145 17th Street N.W.
Washington, D.C. 20036-4688
U.S.A.

Visit us online at www.nationalgeographic.com/books

For information about special discounts for bulk purchases, please contact
National Geographic Books Special Sales at ngspecsales@ngs.org

For rights or permissions inquiries, please contact National Geographic
Books Subisidiary Rights: ngbookrights@ngs.org

Copyright © 2007 National Geographic Society

Text revised from *Race to the Pole* in the National Geographic Windows on Literacy program from National Geographic School Publishing, © 2002 National Geographic Society

All rights reserved. Reproduction of the whole or any part of the contents without written permission from the publisher is prohibited.

Published by National Geographic Society. Washington, D.C. 20036

Design by Project Design Company
Photo Editor: Annette Kiesow
Project Editor: Anita Schwartz

Printed in the United States

Library of Congress Cataloging-in-Publication Data

Thompson, Gare.
  Roald Amundsen and Robert Scott race to the South Pole / by Gare Thompson.
    p. cm.
  ISBN 978-1-4263-0187-2 (library)
  1. Antarctica--Discovery and exploration.
  2. South Pole--Discovery and exploration.
  3. Amundsen, Roald, 1872-1928.--Travel--Antarctica.   4. Scott, Robert Falcon, 1868-1912--Travel--Antarctica.   I. Title.
  G860.T46 2007
  919.8'9--dc22

                    2007007898

Photo Credits
Front Cover: © The Granger Collection, NY; Spine, Endpage: ©   Galen Rowell/CORBIS; 2-3: © Chris Rainier/CORBIS; 6, 8, 16: © Jean-Paul Ferrero/Auscape; 9, 11, 20, 24, 26-27, 29: © Getty Images; 10: ©Michael Maslan Historic Photographs/CORBIS; 12, 33: © Hulton- Deutsch Collection/CORBIS; 13, 19: © CORBIS; 14, 25: © Bettmann/CORBIS; 17: © Library of Congress; 22, 30: © National Library of Norway, Picture Collection; 34: © Colin Monteath/Auscape..

Endsheets: An ice shelf in McMurdo Sound, Antarctica, is illuminated all night during late October when the sun never sets.

Contents

Icebergs tower in the frigid waters along Antarctica's coastline.

Antarctica

This is the story of a race between two explorers. Roald Amundsen and Robert Scott both wanted to be the first to reach the South Pole. To do this, they would have to overcome many dangers.

The South Pole lies near the center of the continent of Antarctica, the coldest and the windiest place in the world. In winter, temperatures can fall below -120°F (-85°C). Howling, icy winds can knock you off your feet. Icebergs, huge chunks of floating ice, make the ocean waters dangerous for ships.

Amundsen and Scott would have to cross the mountains and valleys that shape the Antarctic landscape.

Chapter 1

Meet the Explorers

Amundsen and Scott were going to race across more than 1,500 miles (2,400 kilometers) of frozen land to the South Pole. Who would win?

Roald Amundsen

Roald Amundsen was born in 1872 near Oslo, Norway. Amundsen came from a family of sailors. At the age of 22, he began his adventures at sea. He became an experienced polar explorer. He explored the icy waters far north of Canada.

Roald Amundsen

Inuits living in the Arctic region of Siberia wear heavy parkas to keep warm in the cold climate.

On his sea voyages, he learned a lot about life in the Arctic. He saw how the native people dressed and what they ate to survive the extreme cold. He saw how they used dogsleds to get around.

In 1910, Amundsen set out for the North Pole aboard his ship the *Fram*. Then, he learned that two explorers had already reached the North Pole in 1909. So, Amundsen decided to explore the South

Pole. He knew that Scott was getting ready to explore the South Pole, too. Amundsen sent Scott a telegram telling him that he had changed his plans and was now on his way to the South Pole.

Robert Scott

Robert F. Scott was born in Devonport, England, in 1868. From an early age, he wanted to go to sea. Scott joined the British Navy when he was 14. He trained to be a scientist. As an officer, he led explorations of discovery. He even explored

Robert F. Scott

parts of Antarctica. He spent two long winters in Antarctica on another trip. On that trip, Scott and his team had come closer to the South Pole than anyone had ever been. Now, Scott wanted to return to Antarctica and be the first to reach the South Pole.

Scott was ready to set sail from New Zealand when he got Amundsen's telegram. He was shocked. He had hoped no one else would try to reach the South Pole before he did. Scott decided that he would stick to his plan. He would not let Amundsen shake him. The race was now on.

Roald Amundsen (front row, far left) poses with his crew aboard the *Fram*, which set sail for Antarctica in 1910.

Men and dogs of Robert Scott's expedition team sail to Antarctica aboard the *Terra Nova.*

Amundsen's dogs were Greenland Huskies, a breed especially strong and tireless.

Chapter 2

They're Off!

Amundsen Lands on Antarctica

At first, Amundsen told no one aboard the *Fram* of his change in plans. The crew thought that they were going to the North Pole. On September 9, 1910, Amundsen stopped to get supplies for the expedition to Antarctica. The crew now had fresh water and food for the race.

There were also 97 sled dogs on the *Fram*. These Arctic dogs would prove to be the most important thing that Roald Amundsen brought on his trip.

Finally, Amundsen asked the crew if they wanted to go with him to Antarctica. The men did, and the ship sailed on. They arrived at the Ross Ice Shelf on January 14, 1911, and set up base camp. They would stay there for nine months.

Amundsen had planned every detail of the trip. Over the next three weeks, the team moved tons of food from the ship to the camp. The men also set out food along the trail to the South Pole.

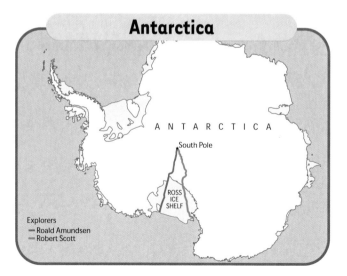

Antarctica

ANTARCTICA

South Pole

ROSS ICE SHELF

Explorers
— Roald Amundsen
— Robert Scott

Equipment and supplies waiting to be sorted and sent to Amundsen's camp.

While waiting for spring and better weather, Amundsen and his men got ready for the trip. They skied and trained the dogs. They looked for ways to lighten the loads that the dogs would have to pull. This would help the dogs go faster.

Amundsen made sure the men ate well to stay healthy and build up their strength. He did not send his men off to explore the area. He did not want them to get hurt or lost. He took no chances.

Scott Lands on Antarctica

Scott set sail from New Zealand on his ship the *Terra Nova*. A bad storm hit the ship on its trip to Antarctica. Some cargo was lost, but Scott sailed on. He landed at McMurdo Sound on January 3, 1911, and set up camp on the Ross Ice Shelf. Scott's camp was not as close to the South Pole as Amundsen's camp. Scott's camp was on the other side of the ice shelf.

Scott arrived with his crew, ponies, dogs, and gasoline-powered sleds. The men used the motor sleds to take the food and supplies to base camp. The first hint of danger came when one of the motor sleds fell through the ice and sank.

By the end of two weeks, the men had built a hut. They had a place to eat and sleep. Scott began to put food along the trail that they would take to the South Pole. They used the ponies and dogs to pull the food. The

Three of Scott's team pose in front of the hut at base camp.

motor sleds did not work in the ice and snow. The ponies tired quickly and were hard to control. Unlike Amundsen's men, Scott's crew did not know how to use the dogs.

Scott and his men explored the area. At times, the men returned to camp tired, frostbitten, and cold. The dogs, tired and hungry, often fought with each other.

Roald Amundsen inspects ice fields near a glacier in the Atlantic Ocean.

Chapter 3

The Race

Amundsen Sets Off

Amundsen set off for the South Pole on October 20, 1911. It was a perfect day. The sky was beautiful and clear. The air was cold, but the men had dressed warmly.

Amundsen and a crew of four men set off with high hopes. They took four sleds piled high with supplies. Twelve dogs pulled each sled. The men had trained the dogs well. They listened to the men's commands.

The men made good time. At their first stop, the men found the supplies they had stored along the route. They fed the dogs blubber, or whale fat, and seal meat.

The dogs hungrily ate their feast. The men ate their meals and slept.

Early the next day, the men left on skis. The dogs pulled the sleds. The men traveled about 13 miles (21 kilometers) per day. It took them about five hours to go that far. Then they stopped.

They built a small mound of stones. Inside the mound they recorded the distance and direction to the next supply of food. The mounds marked the trail. They would need them on the way back. After building the mound, they ate and rested until the next day.

The Amundsen team sets off for the South Pole with sleds pulled by dogs.

Getting Closer

On November 11, they saw mountains. Amundsen named the mountains the Queen Maud's Range after the Queen of Norway. That night they camped at the foot of the mountains. They still had 340 miles (547 kilometers) to go. The men and the dogs began the climb on November 18. Four days later, they were at the top of the mountain.

A howling blizzard set in, trapping them for four days. But the men could not waste time. For the next ten days, the men and 18 of the strongest dogs struggled against strong winds and fog. They fought their way across thin ice that covered deep pits. They kept going.

Finally, on December 8, the sun shone. The men were less than 100 miles (160 kilometers) from the South Pole. The dogs were hungry and tired. The men were almost frostbitten, but still they pushed on.

Amundsen worried that Scott might have already beaten them.

Planting the Flag

On December 14, a cry of "Halt!" filled the air. Amundsen and his men had reached their goal. Each of the men placed a hand on the flag of Norway. They planted it together. Amundsen named the area King Haakon VII's Plateau after the king of Norway.

Amundsen and his men with the Norwegian flag they planted at the South Pole.

One of the ponies Scott hoped would help him reach the South Pole.

The men set up a tent. They took photographs and explored the area. They celebrated with a feast of seal meat. One of the men pulled out cigars. Inside the tent Amundsen left a letter for the king of Norway and a message for Scott. Amundsen had won the race!

Scott Sets Off

Scott set off for the South Pole on November 1, 1911. He traveled with a team of 10 men, 10 ponies, 23 dogs, and 12 motor sleds. Scott hoped all his planning would help him beat Amundsen to the Pole.

Things went wrong almost at once. The men fought constant snowfalls. Temperatures never rose above 0°F (-32°C). The men didn't have the right clothes.

The motor sleds were useless. So were the ponies. The ponies sank deep into the snow and had trouble surviving the cold. But Scott was determined to make it to the South Pole.

First, Scott had to cross the Ross Ice Shelf. Scott and his men marched on foot. Some had skis, but they were no help. Scott's men were not used to skiing.

Half of Scott's 14 man team pull a supply sled.

It took them 15 days to reach the first stop where food had been stored.

Scott led the men on to the next stop. On December 5, the men woke to a fierce blizzard. The snowstorm forced them to stay put for four days. Their sleeping bags were wet. The men were tired and ill. On the fifth day, the men moved on. Two days later, they had crossed the Ross Ice Shelf.

Scott sent the dogs and some of the men back to base camp. Now, the remaining men had to pull the sleds with their heavy cargo.

Reaching the Top

On December 20, the party reached the top of a glacier. The men grew weaker. Every day they battled frostbite, harsh winds, and rugged land. They celebrated Christmas with a meal of chocolate, cookies, meat, and candies.

By January 6, the party was far south. They saw no sign of Amundsen. They hoped that they were beating him. The next few days were hard. Another blizzard hit. Pulling their sleds now seemed harder. Scott knew his men were very tired, but he continued on.

On January 16, Scott and his team were close to the Pole. They thought that they might reach it the next day. Then one of Scott's men spotted a black speck. What was it? The men kept walking. They saw the remains of a camp. It was their worst fear. Amundsen had gotten to the Pole first. The black speck was his flag.

Scott and his team reach the South Pole only to find Amundsen's tent there.

Finally, on January 17, 1912, Scott and his men arrived at the South Pole. A tent with a note from Amundsen was waiting for them. Amundsen asked Scott to get a letter to the King of Norway if he didn't make it back home. Amundsen also told Scott to use anything he and his men had left behind. Scott and his team were disappointed. On January 19, they set off for base camp.

Chapter 4

The Return Trip

Amundsen's Safe Trip Home

Amundsen and his men felt proud as they made their way home. They set out three days after planting the flag. It was a bright, sunny day. Amundsen wanted to get back as fast as he could. He wanted to tell the world that he had been to the South Pole first.

He and his men made good time. They stopped for food at the mounds they had built on the way to the Pole. For most of the trip back, the weather was good. It was cold, but there were no blizzards or big storms.

 Amundsen is honored for being the first person to reach the South Pole.

The team made it back to camp in 39 days. All five men were healthy and happy. Amundsen took the ship back to Tasmania, Australia. The trip took a month. It seemed to take forever.

Upon arriving, Amundsen immediately sent a telegram to his brother. Now the world knew that Amundsen was the first person to reach the South Pole. *The New York Times* reported that "the whole world has now been discovered."

Scott's Last Trip

Scott and his men were tired and cold. They had very little food left, and they had a long trip ahead of them. Scott was not sure if they could make it back to camp.

With little food, the men became weaker and weaker. One man, Edgar Evans, fell on a glacier and hurt his head. He tried to keep going, but he could not. He died in his tent.

Now there were just four men. They walked less and less each day. The weather worked against them. Storms hit. Temperatures fell well below freezing, even in the daytime.

Scott and the men trudged on. They grew weaker by the day. On March 21, 1912, they were only 11 miles (18 kilometers) from a food stop. It would save their lives. But then a blizzard hit. It lasted for nine days. The men could not move. They died in their tent.

Eight months later a search party found the men. They also found Scott's journal and photographs. It tells the tale of their sad trip.

Scott writes in his journal of the expedition to the South Pole.

Tourists visit Antarctica to see penguins and other animals that live in the sea around it.

Antarctica Today

Today, scientists from all over the world live and work in Antarctica. They have set up large stations, that are like small towns. These stations have movie theaters, churches, banks, and hospitals.

The scientists study the weather. They observe the animals in the sea. They watch the ice to see how it changes. Helicopters carry supplies to the scientists who live there.

Antarctica is the only continent that is not a nation or made up of a group of nations. Roald Amundsen may have been there first, but today the South Pole belongs to the world.

How to Write an A+ Report

1. Choose a topic.

- Find something that interests you.
- Make sure it is not too big or too small.

2. Find sources.

- Ask your librarian for help.
- Use many different sources: books, magazine articles, and Web sites.

3. Gather information.

- Take notes. Write down the big ideas and interesting details.
- Use your own words.

4. Organize information.

- Sort your notes into groups that make sense.

- Make an outline. Put your groups of notes in the order you want to write your report.

5. Write your report.

- Write an introduction that tells what the report is about.

- Use your outline and notes as you write to make sure you say everything you want to say in the order you want to say it.

- Write an ending that tells about your report.

- Write a title.

6. Revise and edit your report.

- Read your report to make sure it makes sense.

- Read it again to check spelling, punctuation, and grammar.

7. Hand in your report!

Glossary

base camp   the starting place or headquarters for an expedition

blizzard   a blinding snowstorm with very strong winds

blubber   whale fat

cargo   a load of goods or supplies

continent   one of seven great areas of land on Earth

expedition   a journey taken for a special purpose, such as exploration

glacier   a large piece of ice that moves very slowly down a mountain or across land

iceberg   a large piece of ice floating in the sea

nation   people living in a country under one government

polar   relating to the North or South Pole

research station   place set up by a group for a scientific purpose, such as studying the weather

telegram   a message sent using a code of electrical signals

Further Reading

• Books •

Hooper, Meredith. *Antarctic Journal.* Washington, D.C.: National Geographic Society, 2001. Grades 3–6, 40 pages.

Karner, Julie. *Roald Amundsen: The Conquest of the South Pole* (In the Footsteps of Explorers), New York: Crabtree Publishing Company, 2006. Grades 3–6, 32 pages.

Kostyal, K.M. *Trial by Ice: A Photobiography of Sir Ernest Shackleton.* Washington, D.C.: National Geographic Society, 1999. Grades 5 and up, 64 pages.

Sipiera, Paul P. *Roald Amundsen and Robert Scott: Race for the South Pole* (World's Great Explorers). New York: Children's Press, 1991. Grades 3–6, 128 pages.

• Web Sites •

National Geographic Kids Magazine
www.nationalgeographic.com/ngkids/0002/race_to_ end/

PBS Secrets of the Dead
www.pbs.org/wnet/secrets/case_southpole

BBC British History
www.bbc.co.uk/history/british/britain_wwone/race_pole_01.shtml

South Pole Adventure
http//:astro.uchicago.edu/cara/southpole.edu

Index